P.B. BEAR'S
WORLD OF WORDS

Lee Davis

Family Learning

HOW TO USE THIS BOOK

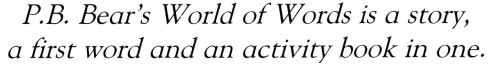

P.B. Bear's World of Words is a story,
a first word and an activity book in one.

Children will love the story of P.B. Bear's balloon ride.
As you read it out loud, they will enjoy matching the
objects in the borders to those in the main pictures
– increasing their vocabulary as they do so.

Each picture is packed with delightful details. The activity
questions can be used as a starting point for enjoying them
as well as to help develop children's observation skills.

Don't forget to look out for the little bear.

Which pages
can you spot
me on?

P.B. BEAR'S DAY

slippers

dressing gown

trousers

shirt

cap

pyjamas

shorts

jeans

sandals

"I have a feeling that this is going to be a very busy day," says P.B. Bear one morning. "What shall I wear?"

4

wardrobe

chest of drawers

socks

handkerchief

pants

waistcoat

scarf

hat

shoes

jumper

Can you point to some of P.B. Bear's clothes that are

○ yellow   ○ blue   ● red   ○ green?

dungarees

T-shirt

rainhat

boots

5

school bag

purse

zip

umbrella

raincoat

sponge

soap dish

soap

hairbrush

beaker

water

mirror

seahorse

bubble bath

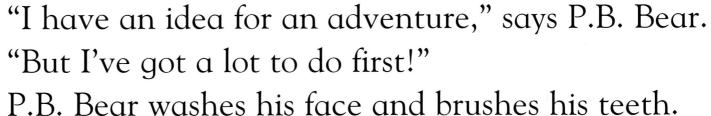

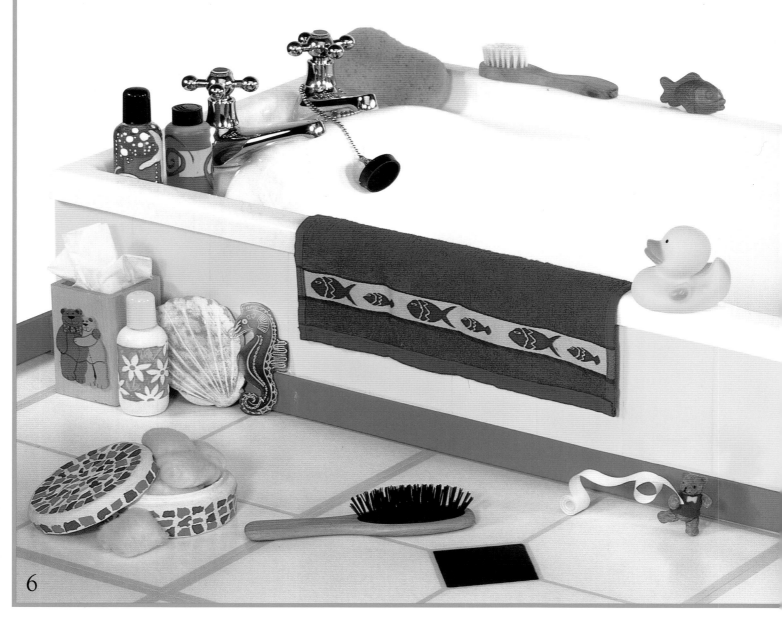

"I have an idea for an adventure," says P.B. Bear.
"But I've got a lot to do first!"
P.B. Bear washes his face and brushes his teeth.
"Now I'm ready to start my busy day!" he says.

6

towel

bath

back brush

taps

comb

flannel

cotton wool

rubber duck

How many bears can you spot in P.B. Bear's bathroom?

How many different brushes can you see?

nail brush

plug

tissues

shampoo

7

basin

toothbrush

toothpaste

cotton buds

sofa

table

cushions

marbles

lamp

clock

toy boat

drawing

"I'm making something special," says P.B. Bear. "Can you guess what it is? It will fly, but it's not an aeroplane or a space rocket!"

- What can you see that makes music?
- What can you see that is used for colouring pictures?

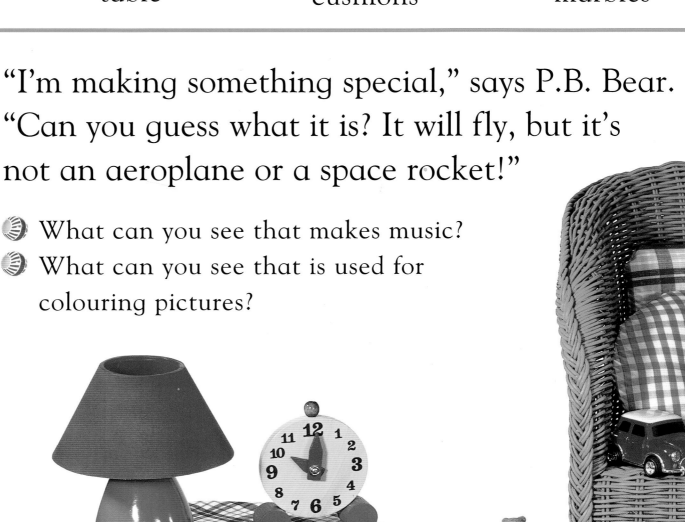

8

paint

paint brushes

scissors

crayons

toy car

playing cards

jigsaw puzzle

drum

horn

blocks

basket

9

coloured pencils

ball

toy mouse

balloon

watering can

basket

daffodils

butterflies

caterpillar

garden rake

trowel

broom

garden fork

P.B. Bear has made a hot-air balloon that will take him on a high-flying adventure. "Ready for take off," he says. "Goodbye garden!"

10

flowerpot

seeds

clippers

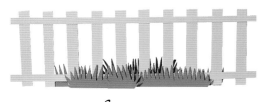
fence

snail

ant

potatoes

lettuces

bean plants

Can you find...
-  1 bird
- 2 butterflies
- 3 lettuces
- 4 daffodils
- 5 ants?

carrots

tomatoes

tree

bird

11

hot-air balloon

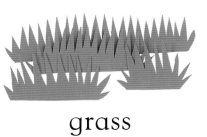
grass

binoculars

camera

tent

fence

cloud

mountains

well

windmill

tractor

caravan

12

farmhouse

barn

bridge

train

village

rabbit

ducklings

duck

cow

The balloon drifts above the countryside.
The animals on the ground look very small.
Can you help P.B. Bear spot . . .

goose

Which animal is crossing the bridge?
Which animal is perched on the fence?

pig

sheep

cockerel

13

cat

horse

frog

bird

chicken

hat

sunglasses

towel

postcards

pencil

sun block

sandwich

Bob

Roscoe

Dermott

Next the balloon travels towards the seaside and lands on the beach.
"Ahoy there, mateys!" P.B. Bear calls out to some friends.

fish

dolphins

starfish

sea

pebbles

rock

seagull

Can you find these shapes at the seaside?

● circle ★ star ▬ rectangle

■ square ▲ triangle

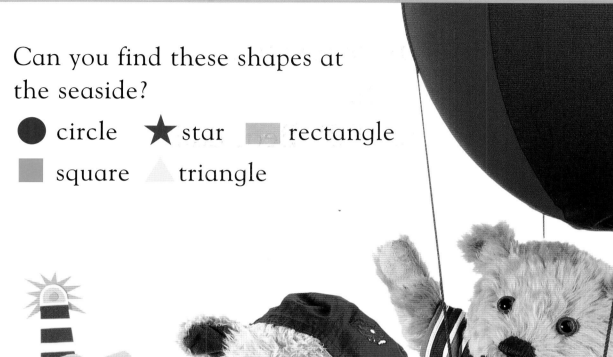

lighthouse

boat

sandcastle

15

spade

sand

seaweed

shells

bucket

waiter

policeman

nurse

fireman

office worker

bicycle

aeroplane

bus

Soon, the balloon is hovering over a bustling street. P.B. Bear looks down on the offices and restaurants, the hospital and the cinema. "What a busy town!" he says.

chair

table

cinema

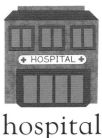

hospital

car

motorcycle

fire engine

postman

letter box

road sign

traffic light

How many nurses can you see?
How many waiters can you see?
How many firemen can you see?

OFFICE

RESTAURANT

HOSPITAL

restaurant

supermarket

café

office block

flower seller

sun

pond

bee

grasshopper

trees

tree house

bench

slide

What is Florrie doing?
What is Dixie doing?
What is Milly doing?

18

skipping rope

seesaw

swing

skateboard

ladybird

lunch box

rucksack

Florrie

Then P.B. sees some friends in the playground.
"Stop and play with us," they call.
B$_U$MP goes the balloon on the seesaw,
before lifting back up into the air.
"I can't stop now!" says P.B. Bear.
"It's suppertime!"

Dixie

Hilda

Milly

19

ball

bats

hoop

Russell

orange juice

butter

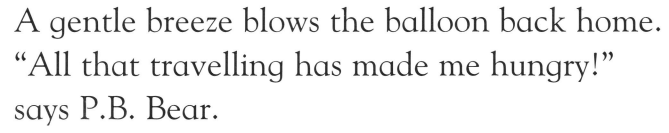

bowl

carrots

celery

honey

bread

ice cream

A gentle breeze blows the balloon back home.
"All that travelling has made me hungry!"
says P.B. Bear.

plates

20

mugs

salt and pepper

washing-up liquid

cupboard

breadsticks

grapes

apple

lemon

cereal

spaghetti

Look at the things to eat in P.B. Bear's kitchen.

 Which are hot? Which are cold?

Which are sweet? Which are sour?

Which are hard? Which are soft?

toaster

brush

dustpan

21

knife fork spoon

kettle

saucepan

cooker

table

rug

torch

friends

lamp

clock

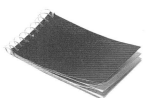

notebook

pen

22

diary

shoes

binoculars

slippers

photographs

camera

telescope

vase

"It **has** been a busy day and now I'm very sleepy," yawns P.B. Bear. "Good night."

daffodils

🌙 Can you remember all the words in P.B. Bear's world?

curtains

moon

window

book

duvet

stars

bed

Where in the world of words would you like to go?

FAMILY LEARNING

Senior Designer Claire Jones
Designers Jeanette Evans
Claire Ricketts
Senior Editor Caryn Jenner
Editor Fiona Munro
Photography Dave King
Illustration Judith Moffatt
Production Katy Holmes
DTP Design Kim Browne

First published in Great Britain in 1998

4 6 8 10 9 7 5 3

Visit us on the World Wide Web at: http://www.dk.com

Reproduced in Italy by G.R.B. Editrice
Printed and bound in Italy by L.E.G.O.

Acknowledgments
Dorling Kindersley would like to thank the following
manufacturers for permission to photograph copyright material:
Ty Inc. for "Toffee" the dog and "Freddie" the frog;
Folkmanis Inc. for the hen puppet;
The Manhattan Toy Company for "Antique Rabbit".

Dorling Kindersley would also like to thank:
Maggie Haden, Richard Blakey,
Vera Jones, and Barbara Owen.

Did you spot the little bear on pages 5, 6, 8, 10, 15, 20 and 23?